FINISH YOUR DISSERTATION BEFORE YOU DIE

The No ABD Solution

Joseph E. Nolan, PhD

Copyright 2016, NTV Resources

Why I Wrote This Book

I would like to thank you for purchasing this book and let me congratulate you for being one of the few to get this far in your education. In the United States only 3% have a doctoral or professional degree.

Surveys conducted by the Council of Graduate Studies (2010) found that 60% of doctoral students who complete all coursework and exams don't earn their degree due to ABD.

The academic job market is tough enough for those who have completed their doctorates. It is almost impossible for ABDs. ABD means "All but dissertation", but in the academic job market, it might as well mean "All but dead"! The purpose of this book is to provide you with the tools and the resources to chart your path and get you through the gauntlet of the doctoral process.

Why You Should Read This Book

Some of you are considering this book because you are at the beginning of your doctoral study and want to chart a path as relatively free of roadblocks as possible. Some of you may be in the middle of your program and are finding yourself mired in fear and confusion, or you may be in the middle of your dissertation and stuck as to where to go next. You may be blocked.

Being stuck is having an effect on you in many different ways:

Health- Both physical and emotional, not finishing has had an effect. You may be getting headaches. You constantly feel this weight on you of this accomplishment that remains unfinished. You find yourself hiding from the project. You just can't walk away from it, but you can't push your way through to completion.

Wealth – As you remain enrolled, your tuition and fees keep mounting. If you walk away, you will still owe the money and if you have student loans, the interest to boot. Finishing is the only way you can turn off that taxi meter of tuition and fees that is constantly running while you remain unfinished.

Relationships – Have you noticed that the longer this dissertation goes on, the less of a friend, or family member you become? They have given you your space, and some slack, but they are getting impatient.

Sex – What's that? Your writing isn't the only thing that's blocked.

Identity – Not finishing is having an effect on who you are. You may feel that you might not be as smart as you thought you were when you started the program. You feel like a poor student, or a poor worker, or fill in the blank here, a poor _____. Whatever, you feel like a failure. This is not what you are. You can show you're better. You can finish this dissertation.

I have supervised dissertations and theses at 6 different universities and have consulted with many students who have found themselves in critical junctures of their dissertation. I have helped students complete when everyone else has given up working with them. I can help you get through your dissertation. YOU CAN FINISH THIS THING!

But I can't do it alone. This book will give you the tools, answer your questions, and allay your fears. Ultimately, however, it is up to you to do the work. Let's click or turn the page and get started.

Table of Contents

Why I Wrote This Book 2

Why You Should Read This Book 3

Table of Contents 6

Chapter 1: Introduction- How to Use this book. ... 12

Chapter 2: The Process 14

Chapter 3: The problem. 15

Chapter 4: Choosing a topic. 17

Chapter 5: The Elevator Pitch 19

Chapter 6: Choosing Your Advisor……………… 20

Chapter 7: Breaking down the Dissertation. 23

Chapter 8: The Research Plan 25

Chapter 9: Pencil Sharpening 27

Chapter 10: Choosing software 31

Chapter 11: Time Management 34

Chapter 12: Writing First Drafts 36

Chapter 13: Blocked? 37

Chapter 14: The Prospectus 39

Chapter 15: The Literature Review 41

Chapter 16: Finding your keywords 42

Chapter 17: Searching the Literature and Delimiting your Hits 43

Chapter 18: Reading the Literature. 45

Chapter 19: Plagiarism 47

Chapter 20: When should you hire somebody? .. 49

Chapter 21: The Proposal Template 52

Chapter 22: Writing Chapter One. 53

Chapter 23: Chapter 1 Introduction 54

Chapter 24: The Problem Statement 55

Chapter 25: The Purpose Statement 56

Chapter 26: Need for the Study 57

Chapter 27: Research Questions 58

Chapter 28: Hypotheses or Objectives 59

Chapter 29: Quantitative, Qualitative, or Mixed Methods? 61

Chapter 30: Definitions of Terms Used in the Study 63

Chapter 31: Basic Assumptions, Limitations, and Delimitations 64

Chapter 32: Summary/Transition Paragraph 67

Chapter 33: The Literature Search 68

Chapter 34: Writing the Introduction to the Literature Review 70

Chapter 35: The Theoretical Framework in the Literature Review 71

Chapter 36: A Thorough Review of Empirical Studies 72

Chapter 37: Summary of the Literature Review ...73

Chapter 38: The Yips 74

Chapter 39: Writing the Introduction to the Methodology 76

Chapter 40: Research Design 77

Chapter 41: Sampling 78

Chapter 42: Population & Sample Participants ...82

Chapter 43: Instrumentation 83

Chapter 44: Surveys 85

Chapter 45: Qualitative Research Classifications 87

Chapter 46: Interviewing 88

Chapter 47: The Role of the Researcher in Qualitative Research. 90

Chapter 48: Information Collection in Qualitative Research 91

Chapter 49: Procedures 93

Chapter 50: Data Analysis 95

Chapter 51: Information Analysis 97

Chapter 52: The Review Process 98

Chapter 53: Handling Revisions............................99

Chapter 54: The Defense - Death by Powerpoint 100

Chapter 55: Approval and the IRB 103

Chapter 56: The IRB 104

Chapter 57: Following the Road Map.................106

Chapter 58: Validity and Reliability.....................107

Chapter 59: Writing the Results Chapter............109

Chapter 60: Writing Quantitative Results...........110

Chapter 61: Writing Qualitative Results.............111

Chapter 62: Mixed Methods Results...................112

Chapter 63: The moment of truth- Answering the Research Questions...113

Chapter 64: Writing the findings or interpretations of results 114

Chapter 65: Generalization 115

Chapter 66: Limitations..116

Chapter 67: Implications 117

Chapter 68: Suggestions for Future Research ..118

Chapter 69: Wrapping it Up 119

Chapter 70: References...120

Chapter 71: Appendices...121

Chapter 72: Dedication and Acknowledgements 122

Chapter 73: Figures, Charts, and Tables............123

Chapter 74: The Table of Contents of the Dissertation..124

Chapter 75: The Defense.......................................125

Chapter 76: Academic Review............................127

Chapter 77: Form and Style.................................128

Chapter 78: Copyright..129

Chapter 79: Publication..130

Chapter 80: Presenting your Work......................131

Chapter 81: Tailoring your dissertation into publishable articles...132

Chapter 82: Publicity and Dissemination of your Research..133

Chapter 83: Using your Dissertation to Drive your Career...134

Chapter 84: Closing comments...........................135

Appendix A: Research Plan Template................136

Appendix B: Dissertation Outline.......................138

About the Author...141

Chapter 1: Introduction- How to Use this book.

First of all, I want to thank you for choosing this book. This is really not a course, per se, in that it has 84 lectures (or chapters) that must be completed in a linear fashion so that you can get a certificate of completion. Rather, the idea is to take what you need. Consider it a user's manual that you can consult any time. In this book, you will find sections on:

Preparing for a line of research
The doctoral process
Choosing an advisor and committee
Navigating red tape
Conducting literature reviews
Formulating your methodology
Collecting data
Writing, presenting, and defending the proposal, and the dissertation.
Motivation and getting unstuck.

I hope that you will use this resource throughout your dissertation process and if you find it useful, recommend it to your colleagues. Thank you, again for making the small investment in this book. Hopefully, it will yield large benefits for you through the completion of your dissertation.

Chapter 2: The Process.

Each university has its own nuances, including preliminary course work, perhaps some directed research under the supervision of your advisor, and comprehensive examinations. However, most programs use the following steps for the dissertation process:

a.) The prospectus

b.) The proposal

c.) The proposal defense

d.) The dissertation.

e.) The dissertation defense

These will all be defined and discussed in upcoming chapters.

Chapter 3: The problem.

All research is predicated on either exploring a problem (or phenomenon), or discovering if something is so, and often, if so, why?

In choosing your topic, you should find a problem or phenomenon that is near and dear to you. This could be from your everyday life: your work: something you experienced: or even something you read. Here is one illustration:

Why can't a winning sports team sell out its stadium, while some losing teams constantly sell out?

This is obviously a problem, at least for the management of those teams that don't sell out their venue.

Here is another:
Al owns a barbeque restaurant in an old established neighborhood. More and more people are coming with friends and asking for vegetarian options. He is also noticing that customer traffic is decreasing radically. Even the regulars are now passing by.

Obviously, Al has a problem, and if he doesn't address it soon. He'll no longer have a restaurant.

Think about these problem statements and relate them to what's going on in your professional life. What problem statement can you come up with? What problem or situation sticks in your craw, or keeps you up at night? Now, think of something that stems from that problem that you would like to study. You can figure why something is, or even offer potential treatments, and/or test those treatments.

Remember, you are not limited to finding out what doesn't work, but you could also examine what does, and why. Also remember that this is your research; something that may carry you through your entire career. Next we will discuss how a problem statement becomes a research topic.

Chapter 4: Choosing a topic.

So, have you thought about a problem, or phenomenon? If you haven't, stop now and think some more. Ok, let's see how your problem translates into a topic.

Remember the sports attendance problem? Let's explore this. Could the reason a team doesn't sell out be due to a team's record? Here is a topic for you that would suggest a Quantitative Methodology.

"Just show me the money: The relationship between team success and profitability."

Or, how about a qualitative methodology?

"Why can't winning teams sell out their games: A Concessionaire's Perspective".

Finally, here is an example of a mixed methodology.

"A comparison of salaries for sports concessionaires in the United States along with corresponding anecdotes on working conditions".

These are all topics that just cry out to be explored. Let's think about YOUR particular topic. Convert it into a one sentence topic statement that you could put on a cover page and we will talk about it more in the next chapter, as you prepare your elevator pitch

.

Chapter 5: The Elevator Pitch

As you begin to take ownership of your research, you will start to talk about it. You will want to have an answer when you are asked about your research. These people may include potential committee chairs, members, grant funders, or employers. You want to have something on the tip of your tongue that you can deliver without confusing or putting people to sleep. Thus, the "elevator pitch".

In under two minutes (the length of the average elevator ride),you should be able to tell people your topic, problem statement, your methodology (Quantitative, Qualitative, or Mixed), your research question(s) and why you feel this research is important to mankind, your field, the community, etc. The more you practice this, the more you will meld with the research, the more confident you will sound, and indeed become. And the more convincing you will be to those you are trying to bring on board as committee members or potential funders.

Please feel free to practice your pitch, bounce off classmates, neighbors, anybody that will listen. Good luck!

Chapter 6: Choosing your advisor.

Probably the most important choice you will make in your doctoral study is the selection of your advisor and dissertation chair. In most programs, these are one and the same. Some students enter a particular school and program to study under a professor who might be considered an expert or has some international renown.

I have mixed emotions about this. While having that professor's signature on your dissertation may have some tangible benefit as far as your earning potential is concerned, it is not without its down side.

First of all, you are in competition with all the other students studying under this advisor.

Second, you may not get along with your advisor. A friend of mine traveled across the country to study under a renowned professor. After moving his family, and two miserable weeks under this advisor, he was told "he wasn't a fit". So off he went, back across the country, to the institution where he earned his Masters degree. Things worked out in the end, however, for he is now a tenured professor at that prestigious university.

Third, you may be considered cheap labor and the professor may not have your best interests at heart.

She may be more concerned with you forwarding her research agenda rather than your own.

It is important that you find an advisor that is interested in facilitating your study and progress.

Some things you must keep in mind when selecting your advisor are:

Do they have the time to work with you?
Do they follow through?
Do you share a common research interest?
Are they interested in you?
What do former students have to say about this professor?
Can you get funding?
How is the professor's health? Do they plan on sticking around this mortal coil?
Have you read any of the professor's work?

Does the professor collaborate well with others?

Many institutions assign advisors by default when a student is admitted, so it is up to you to find out if this professor is right for you. From the minute you enter a program, you should be shopping for a dissertation chair and committee members. We will talk more about committees in a future chapter.

Chapter 7: Breaking down the Dissertation.

Most dissertations consist of 5 chapters. Some programs use 6 with the final chapter being mostly reflective in nature. Creative works and Historical Studies often use a different format containing many chapters. For purposes of this book, we will rely on the 5 chapter format with a generic approach to the format used with most technologies and designs. The 5 chapters are as follows:

Chapter 1- Introduction

Chapter 2 - Review of the Literature

Chapter 3 - Methodology

Chapter 4 - Results

Chapter 5 - Summary and Recommendations

There may be subtle differences in nomenclature, but this is the basic structure. We will go into more detail on every chapter in the following pages.

Chapter 8: The Research Plan

Before you prepare your prospectus, right around the time you come up with your topic and problem statement, you should be thinking up a rough outline, or Research Plan.

The Research Plan should contain the following components:

A brief introduction paragraph which is a statement of fact
Problem Statement: What exists that moves you to explore this topic?
Purpose Statement: Why are you doing this?
Nature of the Study: What are you doing?
Research Questions: What answers do you want to find?
Hypotheses or Objectives
Variables (If applicable)
Population & Sample: Who, where?
Significance of the Study: Why should we care? What is the value to society, to your field?

I will discuss each of these in future chapters. I have included a template in the Appendices so that you can have something to print out or copy and scribble on as you think this through. It won't all come to you at once. So keep it handy so that you are always ready to make a notation.

Considering that you now have a problem statement and topic, you now molding this from just a germ of an idea into a plan for your research.

Chapter 9: Pencil Sharpening

It seems that when we write we spend a lot of time doing all the little transitory things that put us in a frame of mind to write. The problem is that we waste a lot of time while we write instead of preparing ourselves to write beforehand. This is often referred to as "pencil sharpening".

Four things need to be considered. They are:

1.) Your time.

2.) Your space.

3.) Your writing style.

4.) Your tools.

First, let's talk about your time. I'm not talking about time management in general, but the time you allot to your dissertation.

BE SELFISH! This is something that you owe to yourself. Of all the major things you will do in your life, this is the one thing that will live on in history as your creation. You should make this a priority or procrastination will creep in .

GET EVERYBODY ON BOARD! if you have a family, get them to agree to giving you some slack and to help you out with errands and household tasks while you dedicate the next year or two to your dissertation.

DEDICATE AN HOUR A DAY TO DISSERTATION RELATED ACTIVITY. Even if it is just reading articles, or revising and editing your work, keep moving forward. The Japanese have a term that applies here, "Kaizen", which means gradual and never ending improvement. This is a good time to start practicing Kaizen. One way to help you stick to the hour is to schedule it on your calendar, preferably the same calendar that contains the rest of your schedule.

TIME IS $$$$$$! The university will not push you to complete. It is kind of like the fitness center model. They really don't care if you progress as long as the checks are rolling in. In most universities you have a 10 year maximum to completion. All that time, the meter is running. They are collecting your tuition and you're going deeper in debt.

YOUR SPACE:

FIND A PLACE DEDICATED TO WRITING. It may not be home. It might be a coffee shoppe, the library, definitely not your office and not your dining room table.

CONSIDER COMMUNITY WRITING, If you have a buddy working on his dissertation, you may work well as a team. However, you will probably seek solitude to gather your thoughts.

CONSIDER YOUR WRITING STYLE. A first draft is and should be stream of consciousness writing. While you wouldn't want to turn it in, it is important to get your thoughts down on paper or on the screen. You can always edit and revise.

Keep a running Reference page. I am not a big fan of the software program, Endnote, as I have found it to have some style bugs. If you keep your citations and references straight now, you will save yourself some grief later on. Remember that unless you are specifically doing a creative dissertation, there is little room for creativity in research papers. Like the old detective used to say "…just the facts…"

YOUR TOOLS.

Always back up your work. Flash drives, the cloud, your hard drive. Date your filenames so that you are always working on (and turning in) the most current version.

Use reliable computers, and avoid public or your employer's computers. Save your work often. Many word programs now auto save, but don't count on that.

I will discuss software in the next chapter.

If you pay attention to these little items of pencil sharpening, your writing process will sail much more smoothly.

Chapter 10: Choosing software.

Most of you are using the Microsoft Office Suite, which takes care of your Powerpoint and Word functions. If you are doing Quantitative analysis and are very skilled in using Excel, you can enter formulae to analyze your data that you enter on the Excel spreadsheet. For the rest of us there are third party software programs like SPSS (The Statistical Packages for Social Sciences). But what do you need? What's more, when you decide you need it, when should you buy it?

I am going to spend a little time about that now; because timing and decisiveness can save you a lot of money.

Do you need SPSS? SPSS is software designed for input and analysis of Quantitative Data. It can be quite pricey, but you can get a Graduate Student package for 69 dollars for a 12 month subscription (at the time of this printing). Do you need it? You can find out by answering the following questions:

First of all, will you be doing a Quantitative study?

Will you be hiring a stats consultant and/or data entry person? If so, chances are they already have it. If you are hiring a stats person but entering the data yourself, you can enter the data via a spreadsheet program (such as Microsoft Excel), and give the file to your stats person and they can import it to SPSS.

Even if you are running your own stats, you might be able to complete your analysis in 30 days or less. If so, you can use the free trial version. But nowadays, 69 dollars is not bad for an analysis program like SPSS that not only analyzes data according to your variables linked to your hypotheses, but allows you to explore "what ifs" using drop down menus and various selections for variables, groups, and subgroups.

There are other stats programs out there. If you do some exploring you might find some that are open source (i.e. free).

There are also Qualitative Analysis programs out there that basically take open ended responses and establish trends based on pre-identified key words. Among them are ATLAS, QSR, and the open source QDAP.

Finally, there is a program for keeping your citations and references formatted and organized. This program, EndNote, keeps a running reference citation in proper format. It costs about 250 bucks for a single license and has had mixed reviews. As of this printing MS Word and Keynote are offering APA templates for references and citations, but I am not sure how developed they are.

Be sure to check with your university library, Bookstore, or IT department to see if there are discounted or free licenses available as many universities offer them. I have seen copies of Office, End Note, and SPSS at some universities for as little as 10 dollars.

So, in summary:

Make sure you need it.
Do not buy it until you need it.
Do not buy it if you don't know how to use it. (Try it out first, and learn it)

Oh, and those consultants I mentioned? I'll be covering the topic, "When to hire someone" in a future chapter.

Chapter 11: Time Management

In the past couple of chapters, I talked about preparation and the tools to help you along, but how about getting the most out of your time? It's amazing how much time we waste in a day. When you are in the crunch of writing your dissertation, you don't have time to waste. You have time that is taken by work, by family, and community, not to mention, time for meditation or exercise. Yes, the workout is important, for you need to have good health in order for you to handle everything else. What time is left of your waking hours needs to be spent on your dissertation. At least an hour a day should be spent on dissertation related activity (maybe a bit longer on weekends and holidays).
So, how can you insure you have this time? First of all, keep a schedule. Tim Ferris, in his book, "The Four Hour Workweek" has a chapter entitled "The End of Time Management". In it he states among other things that if you prioritize properly, there is no need to multi-task. Try going on a one week media fast. Don't read things you won't use. Practice the art of non-finishing. He advises to avoid

interrupters. Time wasters such as checking email habitually and going to non-mandatory meetings; should be avoided. He also believes that checking mail after lunch and the last hour of the day are the most productive way and warns against checking mail the first thing in the morning. Rather, he proposes posting an auto response informing correspondents of the fact that you only check mail twice a day at designated times, and providing your phone number to reach you in case of a bona fide emergency. I know in my job, nothing is THAT much of an emergency that it can't wait a few hours. He further states that you should strive towards only checking mail once a day. Other tools provided include mastering the art of refusal and how to cut unnecessary phone conversations. Of course you don't want to appear rude, but if you frame everything as your attempt to be more efficient and to provide better service, you will come out the winner and who knows, your efficiency may even be contagious. For more tips, please visit Mr Ferris's website http://fourhourworkweek.com/. Remember, time is money. So it would be well worth your investment to learn how to manage your time a little better.

Chapter 12: Writing First Drafts

Creative writing teachers stress the value of stream of consciousness writing for first drafts. I am proposing that you do the same for your academic writing. Have a template for each chapter with the standard topic headings. Write to get down your ideas. Do not worry about the formatting (APA, MLA, etc.), citations, or typos. The main thing is to get your thoughts down before you forget them. Later, you will go back and fill in your supporting literature, citations, and further expand in the rewrite. The point is that you got your ideas down on paper, and you didn't lose flow by looking up proper APA format or pulling out a text or thesaurus looking for the precise terminology. There is always time to revise, but getting your ideas down is the most important thing.

Chapter 13: Blocked?

You're sitting in front of a blank screen. No matter how you try, you can't get the words to flow. You're blocked! Academic writers and researchers have a little bit of a preventive measure in that there is a fairly standard format of chapters and topic headings in a dissertation. So you always have prompts, even if they are minimal. But still, for whatever reason, be it perfectionism, an overload of literature, or an inability to focus on all the ideas running through our heads, we cannot get things down on paper. There are many resources out there on overcoming writer's block. One famous tip is the 15 minute rule.

Just start free writing for 15 minutes. Go through the topic headings in whatever chapter you are working on, and resolve to write for just 15 minutes. Hopefully, you will get on a roll and continue further. If not, at least you are farther along than you were when you sat down in front of that blank screen. Other tips, these provided by the writing center at the University of Illinois include:

Taking notes whenever you get an idea or thought. Keep it in a pad or on index cards, so that you don't lose the thought before you sit down to write.

Piecework - In our case this means just placing your thoughts under a particular topic heading and not worrying about the chapter as a whole. Again, get those ideas down. I recently had a student who started a blog in her very first research course of all her thoughts, literature citations from all her readings, and reflections toward the topic. The blog can be public or private, but it serves as a running placeholder for everything that has to do with your research for your dissertation, all in one place.

Most of all, recognize the value of a first draft (discussed in the previous chapter). Get it down on paper. Perfection will come later. In fact, your committee will insure that.

Chapter 14: The Prospectus

The prospectus is basically a formal outline of your dissertation proposal. Your prospectus is used to bring committee members on board and provide the university a formal document which displays your research progress within your program. It can also serve as a basis for grant funding. So, what is usually found in a prospectus?

The title.

A brief literature review (usually about 3 pages).

Your research question(s).

Methodology. This should detail how you are going to perform the study.

    a.) How will you select a sample?

    b.) Instrumentation.

    c.) How data will be collected.

    d.) How data will be analyzed

    e.) How the data will answer your Research Questions. (usually about 1-5 pages).

    f.) Timeline. When will you start? How long will it take?

This may be longer and have additional parts (like a proposed budget) if you are seeking funding.

Now you have a solid outline to go by. The broad strokes are here. It's just a matter of shading details in and expanding for your proposal.

Chapter 15: The Literature Review

If you have an early focus on your research topic, every time you do a literature search, be it for a course that requires article summaries or critiques, a course that concentrates on literature searches and analysis, or a literature review course that is directly intended to assist you in preparation of your dissertation chapter containing the literature, everything should focus on that which will assist you in your dissertation preparation.

There are some basic steps:

1. Finding your keywords.
2. Searching the literature.
3. Delimiting (or tailoring) the literature.
4. Reading the literature.
5. Writing the review.

We will cover them, in detail, in the next few chapters.

Chapter 16: Finding your keywords

Keywords are the words you use to search the net, catalogs, and databases. You need to choose wisely. Too much and you can have too wide a range. Miss the mark and you may not find enough literature. Brainstorming keywords based on your topic can be a good start. Think of a concept map. Then start looking at synonyms, antonyms, and variations of root words while you broaden and narrow your terms. When concept mapping for a qualitative study, you should consider using Maxwell's Interactive Model (Maxwell, 2013) or the software program Inspiration (www.inspiration.com). Both of these models will help you come up with useful keywords.

Chapter 17: Searching the Literature and Delimiting your Hits

There are so many data bases out there. How do you know which ones to choose? A literature search should be exhaustive. That means you should at least search all the data bases that pertain to your subject area. I guess you are wondering which databases you should search. If you do not have access to a university library database, you might start with Google Scholar. Scholar will provide abstracts, and sometimes full text articles. From the abstracts you should be able to tell if the article is something that relates to your research topic. This will also give you an idea of how much literature is out there on your topic. You may find out there isn't much. If you have problems finding enough literature, you might consider the technique called "Pearl Growing", where you look in the reference section of articles you have in order to find more articles on the topic for review.

On the other hand, you may find out that your topic has been over researched. That is a sure sign that you may need to either choose a new topic or target a particular population or trait within the topic that indicates a fresh approach. University library online catalogs contain many databases and may also include published dissertations and theses.

One nasty habit that many students have is to only select articles that have a full text PDF readily downloadable. This is the easy, but a sloppy way of doing a search. You should be prepared to find the articles in their journals, and yes, even explore the dusty stacks in that big building with books on your local campus to find the articles you need.

Chapter 18: Reading the Literature.

Once you have gathered all the potential articles, dissertations, books and what not, you are now faced with the monumental task of reading them all. Depending on how much you've found, I am willing to bet that you do not have the time to read everything all the way through, unless you are the greatest speed reader of all time.

First of all, you have read the abstract. That is what led you to pick the article in the first place, right? Now scan the article. DO NOT READ IT ALL THE WAY THROUGH!

Read:

1. The Introduction.
2. Paragraph Headings.
3. First and last sentences of each paragraph.
4. The Conclusion.

From this point you can decide whether the article is still pertinent for your literature review. If not, put it in your discard file, but don't throw it away, yet. Something that doesn't seem pertinent now may be later.

The next step, after you finished scanning the articles, is to return to those articles you have chosen and start taking notes. Use that highlighter, look at the intro, problem statement, Research Questions, Hypotheses,

Methodology, and Results. At a minimum, highlight these features. If you have these common areas identified, it will be a lot easier to write your review. Don't forget to annotate any "aha" statements or findings to cite in your study.

      Having this all at your fingertips will allow you to put together a coherent and comprehensive review. I will discuss the structure of that chapter further on down the road.

Chapter 19: Plagiarism

You may have noticed reports in the media concerning individuals in politics, business, and academia being accused of plagiarism. The accusation alone can threaten a career and render one's research as useless in the academic community.

First of all, let's define plagiarism. The Online Writing Lab (OWL) at Purdue University defines it "as the uncredited use (both intentional and unintentional) of somebody else's words or ideas."

The Council of Writing Program Administrators discusses the causes of plagiarism and gives several tips on how to prevent it in this handout (http://wpacouncil.org/positions/WPAplagiarism.pdf). Many times students plagiarize without being aware of it. They may paraphrase and expand on a particular statement and in crude the bulk of that statement, and then neglect to cite it, or they may just quote a passage and totally forget to attribute it.

On occasion, I have seen students lift entire pages of an article or book chapter and try to pass it off as their own. In most cases, I'll catch it. Usually the language of the lifted material and the rest of the paper (the original thought) just doesn't match up.

There are also software and web based programs out there to combat plagiarism. One of which is turnitin.com . Not only can instructors run your papers through, but you can also do this on your own to test the originality of your work.

      Plagiarism, even when unintentional, can result in you being thrown out of programs, or cost you a career. Take the time to make sure that all the work of others that you use is properly cited and referenced.

Chapter 20: When should you hire somebody?

The dissertation is uniquely your work, but it is an exhibit of your research skills and subject knowledge. Therefore, it is not considered "cheating" to get help with things outside your skillset. Some of those things may be:

1.) Data Entry
2.) Data Analysis
3.) Editing
4.) Coaching

1.) Data Entry: You have all your stats on sheets of paper, or maybe you are entering your data on to a spreadsheet, but you need someone to enter the data into a software program (like SPSS). There are lots of people who do data entry as a sideline or as their everyday job. Ask around your department or campus.

2.) Data Analysis: Your job is to interpret the data that directly applies to your research questions. Anything else is "nice to have" or "gee whiz" information. If helps to have a person that is knowledgeable with a data analysis software program that can perform "what if" analysis and can help you isolate only what's pertinent to your study. Usually those people are Research Associates or maybe even

Graduate Assistants. They can help you interpret the data and even construct your tables. They may even enter your data for a few bucks more. Remember that these are knowledgeable research people and will cost you much more than a data entry clerk.

3.) Editors: While you are responsible for writing your dissertation, it helps to have someone who is a skilled "typist", experienced with academic papers, to clean up your work before submission to your committee. That person should be able to edit your work for grammar, format (APA, MLA, etc), and columns, spacing, and pagination. You may know how to drive your car, but you may not know how to change your oil. This, to me, is the "oil changing" of academic writing. Find yourself a good inexpensive editor. Again, ask around the campus. The person who edited and typed my final draft was my dean's secretary.

4.) Coaches. There are some coaches that serve specifically as personal coaches for people doing dissertations. Some people even make a business of it. When shopping for a coach, you should look for the following:

a.) What can they do for you?

b.) How much do they charge?

c.) Do they get results?

d.) Do they have references?

e.) What is their experience?

      Finally, make sure that you aren't unnecessarily paying for services that can be obtained for free on your campus (from counseling, career advisors, student services, your advisor).

Chapter 21: The Proposal Template

As you probably know by now, the proposal is basically the first three chapters of your dissertation if you are writing a traditional 5 chapter dissertation. The first three chapters
consist of:

    Chapter 1 - Introduction

    Chapter 2 - Review of the Literature

    Chapter 3 - Methodology

In the appendix, I have provided an outline that gives you topic headings so that you can start preparing a rough draft. Please copy it and use for notes as you go through the next few chapters. I will explain each topic heading as I go through it, starting with Chapter 1.

Chapter 22: Writing Chapter One.

As you can see from the outline in the appendix, Chapter One has many component parts. For the traditional dissertation, it generally contains these sections:

Introductory Statement

Problem Statement

Purpose Statement

Need for Study

Research Questions

Hypotheses or Objectives

Nature of Study -Methodology Overview

Definitions of Terms Used in the Study.

Assumptions, Limitations/Delimitations.

Summary/Transition paragraph.

I will cover each of these in detail in the coming chapters.

Chapter 23: Chapter 1 Introduction

The introduction to your dissertation is like any other introductory paragraph in writing. It sets the stage for the chapter and for the dissertation as a whole. It should open with a statement of fact designed to hook the reader. For example:

"There are 1352 guitar pickers in Nashville (Sebastian, 1966)"

The statement should set the stage, be supported by research citations, and logically flow into the next section, which is the "Problem Statement". You should provide a short, well articulated summary of the literature that sets up the study (a few paragraphs), and allude to the fact that the literature will be discussed in more detail in Chapter 2 (The Literature Review).

Chapter 24: The Problem Statement

The problem statement usually describes factors that lead to an identified problem. However, a problem statement may not always address a problem. You could be investigating a favorable phenomenon (e.g. something good is happening) or there might be something in need of improvement. The bottom line is that it should identify a knowledge gap, that is, there is something we need to know that the literature doesn't currently tell us.

Chapter 25: The Purpose Statement

Here you should, as clearly as possible, tell the reader exactly what you are going to do in this study. Discuss it in a general fashion and mention that you will be more detailed and specific in Chapter Three (The methodology).

Example:

"In this mixed methodology study, I will analyze the prior season attendance records of all Major League Baseball, National Football League, National Basketball Association, National Hockey League, and Major League Soccer. The attendance records will be compared to the teams' won-loss records to ascertain correlation. Further, explanations will be provided as to other factors that may have an effect on attendance. A more detailed methodology will be provided in Chapter 3."

Chapter 26: Need for the Study

This section is important for this is where you are "selling" the study. You are telling the reader why they should care about this problem and your research. Here is an example:

"The legendary coach, Vince Lombardi, once said 'Winning isn't everything, it's the only thing.' While winning records are good for attendance, in spite of what Vince Lombardi said, it is not the only thing. This study will explore all the factors that have an effect on professional sports attendance and perhaps provide clues that might help bolster attendance. This study is important to owners, presidents, general managers, and fans who not only want to increase revenues, but also grow the spirit of community by increasing their fan base".

You will provide as much information as possible to explain the significance of the study. What will this study mean in terms of new knowledge generation for your field, your community, and the world at large?

Chapter 27: Research Questions

Before you develop your hypotheses (Quantitative methodologies) or Objectives (Qualitative), you should ask a question or questions about the issue that you posed in your problem statement. These questions will form the basis for your hypotheses or objectives. They should be clear, focused, and should require research and analysis. They should not be answered by easily found facts, or be a simple yes or no answer. Perhaps a guideline to this would be:

If you can get a definitive answer to the question by googling the question, chances are you don't have a strong enough research question to guide your study.

Chapter 28: Hypotheses or Objectives

Depending on whether you will be using a Quantitative or Qualitative methodology, you have either hypotheses for Quantitative, Objectives for Qualitative, and both for Mixed Methodologies. These will flow directly from your research questions. Hypotheses are usually stated as null hypotheses, that is, saying a phenomenon's connection or difference does not exist.

For example:

"There is no significant relationship between immunizations and the prevalence of Autism Spectrum Disorder among children."

-OR-

"There is no significant relationship between participation in college athletics and graduation rates."

The word "significance" is used to denote a statistical relationship exists meaning that a statistical analysis at a predetermined level of confidence will be conducted.

Objectives are usually statements made that outline what will be pursued in order to answer the Research Question(s).

For example:

To ascertain the dietary preferences of supermodels.

OR

To review the training regime of elite junior hockey players.

Depending on your study, you will more than likely have hypotheses or objectives. There are exceptions. The Creative dissertation is one exception and there are others. Discuss this with your advisor to see if your study is one of these exceptions.

Chapter 29: Quantitative, Qualitative, or Mixed Methods?

I've lost count of the times students told me that they were doing a Quantitative, Qualitative, or a Mixed Methods study, when they haven't even constructed a research plan. Let me set this straight so that I can save you a lot of unnecessary hassle.

YOUR RESEARCH QUESTIONS SHOULD DRIVE YOUR METHODOLOGY, NOT THE OTHER WAY AROUND!

You shouldn't be designing the response to your problem statement with your Research Questions, hypotheses, or objectives based upon the type of methodology with which you feel the most comfortable. First of all, research should bring you a bit out of your comfort zone, and perhaps most importantly, you should use the methodology that will provide the most comprehensive and exacting answers to your research questions.

So, establish your problem statement, compose the Research Questions, and the hypotheses or objectives that will answer those questions. At that time, the how, your methodology, will become evident.

Chapter 30: Definitions of Terms Used in the Study

The Definition of Terms is basically a glossary for those who are not fully familiar with your topic. Consider that you probably have a subject matter expert on your committee who is familiar with all the jargon. This most likely means that two committee members, and those up and down the line who will be reading your research, may not be. Thus, the need for a Definition of Terms section. This dictionary or glossary formatted section will define terms, acronyms, etc. as they are used in your study. Remember, the textbook definitions and how they are defined in your study may differ. So be clear.

Chapter 31: Basic Assumptions, Limitations, and Delimitations

The basic assumptions of your study are the givens. What is generally accepted to be true. There are four kinds: methodological, theoretical, topical, and measures.

Methodological:
General universal research assumptions that have been made for generations before you.
Examples:
For Interviews and surveys, we assume the participant is telling the truth. Reading levels of participants might be another example.

Theoretical:
Theoretical assumptions are usually made evident in your theoretical construct and will more than likely be mentioned in your theoretical framework. Basically, your theory will make certain assumptions.

Topical:

The previous research on your topic may have had topic specific assumptions. They should be uncovered in your literature review.

Measures:
The measures that you will use will come with its own set of assumptions. If a formal measurement instrument is used, for example, one might assume that the standard administration protocol for that instrument would be used.

Limitations and Delimitations are often confused with each other, so much so that you often only see limitations listed in dissertation proposals. Limitations are mostly things that cannot be investigated because it is beyond your control. For example, sample size. You would like to have 200 participants in your study, but you could only round up 100, for whatever reason. In contrast, a delimitation would be something within your control. For example, an observation period might be limited by time constraints. After all, you want to get this dissertation finished!

Often studies, especially Qualitative ones, tend to have limitations and delimitations arise during the course of the study. Obviously, they can't be predicted in Chapter 1, so you would discuss them in the final chapter, your conclusions (more than likely, this will be Chapter 5).

Chapter 32: Summary/Transition Paragraph

In order to keep your reader's interest, and to motivate them to dig further into your study, you should occasionally remind the reader where they are. The adage "Tell them what you are going to tell them; Tell them; Tell them what you told them; " is appropriate for any story, presentation, or research paper. Although Chapter 1 falls under the "Tell them what you are going to tell them" part, each chapter is basically its own story with an Introduction, Body, and Conclusion. That being said, you should provide a nice wrap up in the form of a summary paragraph ("Tell them what you told them") while letting the reader know very briefly what is going to be contained in subsequent chapters (again, "Tell them what you are going to tell them") It provides a smooth transition and a tease into your next chapter.

Chapter 33: The Literature Search

When I was a graduate student, things were a lot different than they are now. Thesis students were expected to conduct "an exhaustive search". While this is still the case the search process was much more difficult "back in the day". The online data bases that we take for granted today did not exist, at least to the extent we see today. We were often limited to whatever our university library had available. Literature was found either in physical stacks of journals, in microfilm or microfiche copies. The search procedure was time consuming, and expensive. I remember most the times that I went into the stacks, found the journal article I was looking for, and finding myself more interested with either the article before or after, reading that totally unrelated article, and generally wasting hours of time.

Now you can focus a little better in your "exhaustive search". One thing to keep in mind, however, is that you should not only limit yourself to those articles that are available in full text. If an article is important for your study, then have your library order it, even if it costs (the university or you) a few dollars.

When searching the literature, how do we know what's pertinent? As I discussed in an earlier chapter, read the abstract. If it looks pertinent from the abstract, print or copy the article. Once you have a collection of articles, scan them (in other words, read them lightly). If an article still seems pertinent, read it more fully. Pick out what supports or disagrees with your research. Highlight those points and write notes on each copied article. In another chapter, I will discuss how to organize this literature when writing the review.

Chapter 34: Writing the Introduction to the Literature Review

The introduction to the Literature Review should be a preface that sets up the chapter. When one looks at what enhances the validity of the study, the ability to replicate is considered a hallmark. Therefore, the introduction should at least mention the keywords used, the databases included in your search and the years covered. Committees may or may not agree with this, but it only enhances your study. The rest of the introduction should flow logically into the body of the review.

Chapter 35: The Theoretical Framework in the Literature Review

The review is usually written in one of two forms. Either it is topically based on the keywords or phrases, or it could be in a narrative form that flows logically. This tends to be a little trickier in my opinion. Whichever way you (or your chair) decides, you will need to discuss the theoretical framework that guided you in choosing your methodology. This usually consists of literature of scholars who were pioneers of this chosen methodology. While it need not be exhaustive or lengthy, it should provide solid rationale for your choice.

Chapter 36: A Thorough Review of Empirical Studies

What encompasses a thorough review? According to the University of Toronto library, a literature review must do four things:

1.) Be organized around the thesis or research questions.

2.) Synthesize results into what is and is not known.

3.) Identify areas of controversy.

4.) Form questions that may require further research.

In short, it should set up your story. A literature review should be differentiated from an Annotated Bibliography which is more concise and evaluative in nature. One thing that varies in literature reviews is the length. They tend to vary with each committee. But, above all, bear in mind the word, "Exhaustive".

Chapter 37: Summary of the Literature Review

Summarizing the chapter can take as little as a paragraph or two. Mostly, you want to include a nice wrap-up of the literature reviewed and present how it applies to your study. Then provide a nice transition into how you are to go about this process in the next chapter, Chapter 3, the Methodology.

Chapter 38: The Yips

As you get deeper and deeper into this study, you may start feeling an overwhelming sense of dread. I have decided to take some time out here to address it. The Yips is a sports term. Wikipedia defines it as "the apparent loss of fine motor skills without apparent explanation… "

Athletes affected by the yips demonstrate a sudden, unexplained loss of previous skills. Athletes affected by the yips sometimes recover their ability, sometimes compensate by changing technique, or may be forced to abandon their sport at the highest level.

Have you come to a point in your research where you are stuck, feel like you have no place in Doctoral Study, or have lost confidence in your skills? You, my friend, basically have the research version of the yips. For you, abandoning "your sport" is probably not an option. So, you can either "recover your ability" or "compensate by changing technique". One way to accomplish this is to just work or as a famous athletic apparel maker used to say, "Just do it".

Resolve to spend an hour a day doing something related to your dissertation, be it literature search, reading articles, editing previous writing, or writing something new in a stream of consciousness first draft form. You can always go back and edit. The point is you can sit on the couch paralyzed or you can just do something related that will kick start you to overcome those yips. If you can't do this all by yourself, go talk to someone. It can be a friend, research colleague, faculty member, life coach, or counselor. Anyone can give you a push. You have come too far to stop now. Onward and upward over the yips.

Chapter 39: Writing the Introduction to the Methodology

The Methodology is basically a play by play that answers those five timeless questions: Who? What? Where? When? How? But before you jump into it, you should ease the reader into the study by restating the purpose of your study and the theoretical construct that guides it. Then you are ready to move into the nuts and bolts of your research.

Those 5 questions phrased in terms of the methodology are:

Who are the study participants?

What are you doing exactly (intervention, observation, etc)?

Where are you going to do it?

When will you conduct the study?

How are you conducting the study, in detail. (collecting and analyzing your data).

This is basically the framework of the chapter. The rest is shading in the details.

Chapter 40: Research Design

This is the section where you discuss the theoretical basis for your design, and why you chose this type of design to answer your rescarch question(s) in addition to specifically outlining the type of methodology. Depending on whether you are conducting a qualitative, quantitative or mixed methods study, there are several different designs to choose from; much too many to mention here. Your research questions, your hypotheses or objectives, will dictate what type of design you use. Your methodologist, a member of your committee, can help you choose the design. Again, when in doubt, consult your committee chair.

Chapter 41: Sampling

When conducting a particular research method, quantitative research in most cases, one cannot obtain data from an entire population. So systemic procedures exist to collect data from a smaller representative segment of that population. That procedure is known as sampling. A sample can be a group of participants, treatments, situations, selected from a larger population.

There are several ways to select samples. The most well known, within quantitative circles, would be random sampling. However, there several variations of this:

Stratified – a sample with representative groupings of the whole. For example-

Your population is a school of 2000 students. Out of those two hundred students it is determined that the following percentages fall into these social groups:

Nerds – 20%

Jocks – 10%

Cool Kids – 30%

Invisibles – 40%

If you were to select a sample of 200 students, a stratified sample would be represented based on those percentages. In other words 40 nerds, 20 jocks, 60 Cool Kids, and 80 Invisibles. You would still select your participants randomly but you would cap your recruiting in that social group as each group filled up.

Systemic – Let's say that you were a philanthropist in the year 1960, and you decided you were going to give a million dollars to .1 % of the population. You were going to select them by going through the Miami telephone book. The best way to randomly select the winners would be as follows:

Miami population in 1960 = 290000 (approx.)

Sample of 290 candidates

290000/290 = 1000

Select every 1000th person

Of course, this wouldn't be completely random, as not everyone was listed in the phone book. That would be a limitation (See limitations and delimitations in Chapter 31.)

Cluster- A cluster sample is a randomized sample of groups, but selecting all the participants within that group. For example,

There are 100 classrooms in a building, 10 rooms are randomly selected, everyone in each room participates.

These are just a few of the randomized sampling techniques available to you.

Non randomized sampling includes:

a.) Quota samples – Let's say you need 120 students for a student anxiety survey.

- 30 education majors
- 30 engineering   "
- 30 nursing   "
- 30 business   "

Participants are recruited until the quotas are filled.

b.) Purposive samples – Example - A teacher wants to conduct a study
at a school known for a student body with exceptional skills and talents.

c.) Samples of Convenience - In this case, you usually just recruit participants, via the web, or a bulletin board. You may offer an incentive for participation.

d.) Snowball sampling.- Here you are using participants as sources to bring in other qualified participants for the study.

Detailed descriptions of all the above and the differences between them can't be adequately explained in a short chapter, and it is not the intent of this book to supplant a good research methods course. Your Research Methods textbook can provide you much more information. In summary, you should keep in mind that:
-Random samples are not always possible
-You will probably choose the treatment.

There are usually situational limitations that dictate your use of sampling. You don't have to be perfect. The sample selection only needs to be good enough to achieve your purpose.

Chapter 42: Population & Sample Participants

When working on the methodology, the old "who, what, where, when, how" questions apply.

Who are you studying? People, animals, archives?

What are the demographics?

What will you be doing?

Will there be an intervention or treatment, interviews, surveys, reviews of existing data or studies?

Where are you going to get the participants from?

When will you perform the data collection and for how long?

How are you going to recruit and screen your participants?

All this should be explained in a few paragraphs.

Chapter 43: Instrumentation

Depending on the type of information you are trying to ascertain, you may have the need for instrumentation. There are several different types. Examples include:

a.) Formalized norm referenced instruments- These are instruments that have been tested among a large population, with a variety of characteristics, and quantitatively analyzed to establish predetermined scores. These scores would classify the participant into a certain subset. For example, the Stanford-Binet is a norm referenced IQ test. Some tests may establish a student's aptitude normed to a certain grade level.

b.) Formalized inventories – An inventory may not be norm referenced, it could be designed to determine interest in a certain occupation, or activity. The questions are designed and may even be piloted for validity, but they are usually not statistically normed against a large population.

c.) Surveys or questionnaires – These are fact finding instruments, designed to answer specific Research Questions. They can be quantitatively based (i.e. using Likert scales) or qualitative (using open ended questions).

d.) Scripted Interviews – Interviews are intended to draw out qualitatively based open ended answers. In order to prompt unbiased, reliable information, they are scripted, so that the questions are always asked in the exact same order, and manner.

If you are using a formalized instrument (norm referenced or not), you should have permission from the author or publisher to use it. In most cases the purchase of the instrument comes with that permission. However, if you want to use only part, or adapt the instrument, you must get permission to do so.

Surveys or questionnaires may or may not be copyrighted. Check in each case to see if you need permission to use it. Often, it is necessary to design your own interviews or surveys. There are a lot of good books out there to help you compose them. Depending on the exactitude required, you might want to perform a pilot study to see if the instrument does what it is supposed to do in terms of yielding the required data. The bottom line is that the instrument should provide the answers to your Research Questions.

Chapter 44: Surveys

When gathering data, you may find that the best way to get the information you need is through a survey. Surveys are usually self designed, consisting of closed ended questions which will yield codable answers capable of analysis. Closed ended questions are usually associated with Quantitative studies, while open ended questions would more likely yield qualitative information.

There are several general types of survey methods. They are:

Face to Face

Telephonic

Mail or email

Online (Survey Monkey, Google forms, Zoomerang, for example)

You have probably taken a survey at some time in your life; a census, political poll, or one of the marketing surveys conducted by those people with the clipboards in the mall.

One of the key characteristics to a successful survey data collection is a high response rate. This applies generally to mail or email surveys. When you conduct surveys over the phone or face to face, response rate is usually not a problem. There are some modes of data collection that have a higher expectation of participation than others:

Direct administration (captive audience)

Door to door (not so much)

Direct mail (depends on how many rounds you mail).

Email/web (depends on exposure)

Telephone (depends on your tenacity and your reaction to rejection)

When performing quantitative research with closed ended surveys (containing Likert scale quantitative, or multiple choice, true/false items), completed surveys are crucial. Open ended surveys (containing essay type questions) for qualitative research, however, grant a little more latitude.

Chapter 45: Qualitative Research Classifications

Quantitative research methodologies are often variations on the same theme. Qualitative research, however, is about as open as the objectives of your study. For every research question there is a methodology that will yield the desired information. Here are a few examples. John W. Creswell, a guru of research methodologies, both qualitative and quantitative, outlines five different types of qualitative research: Narrative, Phenomenological, Grounded theory, Ethnographical, and Case Study.

Narrative focuses on an individual, possibly a portrait.
Phenomenological obviously studies a phenomenon, or series of events.
Grounded theory explores a theory.
Ethnographic usually studies a culture sharing group.
Case Study usually studies an individual case involving an individual or small group.
While the foci seem self explanatory, the methodology, and meanings would be better explained by the methodologist on your committee, chosen by you. Make them earn their money. Ask questions!

Chapter 46: Interviewing

The key to good interviewing is to have good open ended questions that will spur the interviewee to answer with something more than just a "yes or no". If you were to be content with yes or no answers, then you could have used a survey. Starting your questions with "How, where, or why" is more likely to bring more expansive answers. Ask one question at a time and LISTEN to the answer before asking any follow-ups for clarification. Keep your questions brief. It's not a lecture and it's not about you. Don't push the response. Let the interviewee think about her answer. Don't worry about dead air pauses.

Don't interrupt, but if the interviewee strays from the question, you can bring them back on point with a follow up.

Don't switch the recorder off and on. The distraction might cause the interviewee to lose his train of thought. End the interview at a reasonable length. I tend to think a half hour is about the best to hope for, but you may have just a few participants allowing you to be able to have a more in depth session, or conversely, you may have a number of participants that might make brevity necessary in order to involve everyone.

Keep interviews 1 on 1. A group interview is more of a focus group and will definitely yield different answers than the more pointed one on one.

Good luck with your interviews.

Chapter 47: The Role of the Researcher in Qualitative Research.

In your methodology chapter you are expected to describe your role in the protocol and information collection process. In Qualitative research, the researcher is basically the instrument of information gathering.

In this chapter you should describe your role in recruitment, selection of participants, conducting the interview, transcribing, and analyzing the information gathered. If you have assistance in any part of the process, you need to mention it. Don't forget to include your interview questions either as a figure in the chapter or as an appendix at the end after the references.

Chapter 48: Information Collection in Qualitative Research

Depending on the type of Qualitative research you are conducting, you may have different forms of information collection. Here are a few examples:

For **narrative research**, you will primarily be drawing from interviews and documents.

In **Phenomonological** studies, you may use interviews, but might also draw from documents, observations or art exhibits.

For **Grounded Theory** you will be conducting interviews with multiple individuals. How many? Qualitative Research guru, John Creswell, believes as many as 20-60. Your committee may have a different idea, however.

In **Ethnological** studies you tend to rely on observations and interviews but you might draw from other sources as you spend more time in the research setting.

For **Case Studies**, you would also use interviews, observations, documents, and artifacts.

While other lesser known approaches may require different sources, the interview and/or observation will probably play the predominant role in gathering your information.

Chapter 49: Procedures

As I have previously mentioned, a hallmark of a valid study is the ability to replicate it. This portion of your chapter is dedicated to setting down exactly, step by step, your protocol for the study. If you are doing basic research with an intervention or treatment, you should outline it step by step, so that the protocol can be followed, and understood. If you are doing applied research, every step of the data collection procedure, in order, should be described. Here is an example from my study on Relative Age Effect and success in the National Hockey League:

Procedure

The birthdates and countries of birth were entered by month into SPSS for windows, version 12.0 under the following variables Team, Month of Birth, and Country of Birth. The frequency distribution was compared to the live births in Canada over the course of a year. These data were obtained from Statistics Canada – Birth and Deaths of 1985 and reflected the number of live births, by month, from the period Jan 1 – Dec 31, 1985. These figures compared with the figures from Barnsley et. al. (1985), live births from July 1, 1966- June 30, 1967 are shown in Table 1. The year 1985 was chosen as it reflects the modal birthdates for

Canadian born players in the junior hockey leagues sampled (85.5 % of the OHL and WHL rosters combined).

Chapter 50: Data Analysis

In Quantitative studies or for the quantitative portion of Mixed Methodology studies, this section of the Methodology chapter is dedicated to providing a description of how you are going to analyze the data you have collected. You should discuss what form of software, if any, that you might be using (e.g. Excel or SPSS) and how it will be used to provide your results that will be presented in Chapter 4 (the Results Chapter). You would also provide information on how the data will be analyzed, stored, and protected to safeguard the privacy of the participants.

Here is the Data Analysis breakdown from the study mentioned in the previous chapter:

The first analysis was performed on the birthdates of players in the National Hockey League. These figures are shown alongside Barnsley et. al. (1985) in Table 2. Data from Table 2 representing quarterly frequencies in total and by country have been graphed and are presented in Figure 1. While a quarterly comparison shows that the relationship has flattened slightly between 82-83 and 03-04, 8.8% more players were born in the first quarter than in the last.

We then extended the review to WHL players (table 3) and OHL players (table 4). Again, the relationship has flattened slightly, but not to the extent of the NHL. The 03-04 data reflects that a WHL player is over 3 times as likely to be born in the first quarter of the year as the last, and a OHL player, almost 4 times as likely.

As you can see from the use of tables, the data is presented through the tables and then the tables are interpreted in paragraphs surrounding them in the results. This will be further discussed in the Results chapter.

Chapter 51: Information Analysis

Information, in Qualitative studies, tends to be more voluminous than data portrayed in Quantitative studies. So it is important that you have rules and procedures in place for assembling the information, organizing, dissecting, and storing it. Many people use software to identify trends, keywords, or common threads in the information gathered. (e.g. NVivo).

Once these processes have been decided upon and outlined, the methods of storage and protection of the information should also be described. Finally, a description as to how this will all be presented in the Results chapter should be alluded to.

Chapter 52: The Review Process

This is a difficult subject to chat about because each program has its own nuances. I will try to give you my insight based on systems that were in place at the 6 universities I have had the pleasure of working with.

Let's start with the proposal. After you have it written, you submit it to your committee chair. She will review it and may either have you do revisions, or just approve it for the other committee members to review. Some chairs prefer all members to review at once so that comments can be combined and the ideas for revision can be delivered in one voice.

After your revision, the chair will either call for further revision or schedule a proposal defense meeting. This will be discussed in the next few chapters.

Chapter 53: Handling Revisions

One of the main reasons to have a committee that works well together is to insure a smooth review and revision process. If you prepare a revision based on comments, you need to be sure that the changes you make for one committee member does not put you offside with another committee member. This is why I suggest that if there is no rule in place, you get the chair's assurance that he will arbitrate conflicts and have the final word, thus saving you from bouncing back and forth trying to appease individual committee members.

Chapter 54: The Defense - Death by Powerpoint

Have you ever had the experience where you were sitting in an auditorium, looking at slides that were so busy that you could figure out the wiring diagram, no matter how long the presenter explained it? Or you found yourself wondering if somebody had to pay a ransom to get you released as the presenter describes, in a monotone, slide 178. Or you strain your eyes to read text that bled into the background. If you have, then you have to some degree, experienced death by powerpoint.

Some people believe that no powerpoint is good powerpoint. However, there are times when a powerpoint presentation is appropriate and times when it is not. Salmon Khan of Khan Academy fame uses, not a powerpoint, but the equivalent of a smart board to present mathematical, scientific, and statistical information in a step by step manner. For him, a standard powerpoint presentation wouldn't work.

When you are in a small group, in person, such as your dissertation committee, you are probably going to be having a bit of dialogue back and forth. Your committee members may want to take notes, so here, a handout would be a much better tool than a powerpoint projected on the wall or passed around the table on a tablet.

If you absolutely must use a powerpoint presentation, the presentation slides should be simple. You should be the focus of attention. Your slides are there to reinforce your points, nothing more. Garr Reynolds, in his book "Presentation Zen", uses the term "Slideumentation" to describe slides with so much verbosity that a person could just come in and get a copy of the slides and have pretty much the same thing as if they sat through the presentation. Slides are not cue cards. They are not your script. They are supporting material.

If you ever get the chance. Watch two presentations on Youtube; one by Bill Gates, and one by Steve Jobs. You will notice that Gates uses a lot of Slideumentation while Jobs let the product and his emotion sell the presentation. The slides were just there to add impact. That is what you should strive for.

Media expert, Guy Kawasaki, has a rule for effective presentation. He calls it the "10-20-30 rule" No more than 10 slides (12 if you count title and reference slides). The presentation should be no longer than 20 minutes. People tend to zone out after that. Finally the text should be no smaller than 30 point font, especially if you are presenting in a large auditorium.

Be kind to your committee and your audiences. Don't inflict "Death by Powerpoint".

So, when it comes to your defense meetings. It is up to you to let your work speak for itself, and to provide your committee just a little memory jogger in terms of an overview. They have already read your work, and if you have gotten to this point, you probably already have their approval. Although they may need the rest, don't provide them any opportunity to nap during your meeting.

Chapter 55: Approval and the IRB

Once you have completed your proposal meeting and have obtained the committee's approval, depending on your program, you may have a Dean's review or an Academic Reviewer perform an additional review of your proposal before you have the final approval to move on. The reviewer may require further revision. Stay close with your chair during this process. Once that is done and your proposal is finally approved, you can then move on to preparing your application for the Institutional Review Board (IRB), if it is required.

In most cases, some degree of IRB approval is required. It will be discussed in the next chapter.

Chapter 56: The IRB

The Institutional Review Board or IRB is a committee put together to protect human subjects. There are varying levels of review based on the type of population being studied or data collected. The most prominent being Full, Expedited, or Exempt.

Full review is required when you may have an intervention or some kind of data collection effort using vulnerable populations (e.g. individuals with disabilities, veterans, prisoners, minors).

Expedited review usually includes some kind of data collection effort that entails no intervention, but rather a survey or interview where privacy and confidentiality is insured, and where none of the participants are from a vulnerable population. This process may require just as much paperwork, but is generally questioned less stringently by the board.

Finally, the exempt review occurs when someone is collecting archival data or any study that does not involve direct human contact. It generally requires less paperwork and is not reviewed formally by the entire board, usually it is reviewed by one designated member of the board.

The board meets periodically. When your study gets to the board, they may approve immediately. They may have questions or they may require a change in methodology before approval. The application form can be quite lengthy, some being about 30 pages, but most of the information can be cut and pasted from you prospectus or proposal. Once you have IRB approval, you can go forth with your study, recruit subjects, provide interventions, and collect data. It is important to remember that you cannot recruit subjects, provide interventions, or collect data until you have IRB approval.

Chapter 57: Following the Road Map

When you put together your proposal, especially when outlining your methodology, you provided yourself a road map. You presented your problem statement, asked your research questions, and based on that, formed your hypotheses and/or objectives. Now you will take the data you collected, match them to those hypotheses and/or objectives in order to answer those questions. Perhaps the most difficult part is sorting the data and information which is pertinent to the Research Questions and that which is just nice to have. When writing your results chapter, you will be called upon to separate the wheat from the chaff, so to speak, to present only those findings that make sense in answering the research questions. Hopefully the following chapters in this section will aid you in doing that.

Chapter 58: Validity and Reliability

When we speak of validity in its purest sense, we mean "accuracy". Are your findings accurate? Do they answer the questions you posed? Are they generalizable to other settings or populations? In other words, will you find the same answers in similar circumstances in other populations, larger populations, and at other times or situations?

In order for a measure to yield valid results, it must be reliable, that is, basically consistent within the measurement. If any bias occurs, the measure cannot be completely reliable. Are all the participants in a study getting the same amount of sleep? Are they getting the same diet? Are any on medications or suffering with allergies? Is everyone putting forth the same amount of effort? Is the testing environment the same for everyone? Is the person recording the data seeing things the same way as the next recorder? All these are forms of bias. Participant error and bias, observer error or bias, or systemic bias may occur and should be discussed in the final chapter of your dissertation as possible weak points in your study. Does this mean your research was of no value, or considered a failure? Of course not. It just means that these points should be considered when a reader interprets or applies your results.

Chapter 59: Writing the Results Chapter

In the five chapter traditional dissertation, Chapter Four is designated as your results chapter with Chapter Five reserved for discussion and conclusions. Therefore, Chapter Four should only contain the data analyzed to answer your hypotheses and/or objectives. In Quantitative studies, it is a little more cut and dry than Qualitative or Mixed Methods. In the next two chapters, I will outline how to write up each method's results.

Chapter 60: Writing Quantitative Results

Sifting through the data to find out what is pertinent to report is probably the most difficult part of the study. Writing quantitative results is comparatively easy, however. You have tables that are constructed from the data you analyzed. You will probably begin with a demographic table breaking down pertinent characteristics of your population, Gender, Race, Age, etc; anything that is pertinent to your study. Next you will assemble tables that address your hypotheses.

The tables should show the measures of central tendency, or other information that shows the significant result (or insignificance). Under each table you will present a word picture of what is depicted in the table and how it bumps up against the hypothesis.

When you have addressed all the hypotheses, you will summarize in a few paragraphs whether each hypothesis is accepted or rejected.

Voila! The results chapter is complete.

Chapter 61: Writing Qualitative Results

Writing your results for a qualitative study can be a little more detailed and might require a bit more creativity than with a quantitative study. While you want to provide no more information than what answers your research questions, you may find yourself providing copious amounts of information to fully answer each question, depending upon the mode you used for collection.

In the case of interview, rarely do you provide entire transcripts. Instead you tend to highlight those key points that address your research question. You might use a software program like "NVivo" which groups like comments in interviews and identifies trends, thus making the analysis and reporting less cumbersome.

The main thing to remember is that the results chapter is just for reporting, not discussion or opining. That you will do in the final chapter.

Chapter 62: Mixed Methods Results

Mixed Methods reporting combines all the intricacies of Quantitative Methods with the detailed descriptiveness of the Qualitative. You either have primarily Quantitative or primarily Qualitative. The Research Questions must still be answered, though you will be addressing both hypotheses and objectives in the results.

It is important when you design your study that you ascertain that the research questions can only be answered by conducting a mixed methods design, not just by either Quantitative or Qualitative methodologies alone.

Chapter 63: The moment of truth- Answering the Research Questions

As you analyze your data, if you designed your study correctly, you will find that information gathered will directly match up to your research questions. Sometimes a group of questions combined might provide the answer, sometimes one source provides the answer. Your committee methodologist can best provide guidance in this area. If you performed a quantitative study, you will answer the research questions by accepting or rejecting each hypothesis. If you performed a qualitative study, accomplishment of your objectives is predicated on answering those research questions. A mixed methods study will necessitate addressing both hypotheses and objectives.

Chapter 64: Writing the findings or interpretations of results

The final chapter takes all the results you reported in the previous chapter and wraps them up. You explain what they mean in terms of answering your research questions. How they match up to your literature you reviewed in Chapter Two, and what they mean in terms of relevance to your field, the theoretical arguments, and the research community as a whole. You'll also explain how the research can be used in other contexts and set the stage for future research along this line.

Chapter 65: Generalization

In your final chapter, you should address the possibility of generalization.

Generalization is how your methodology might be used in a different context, or with a different population. In some cases, it might be an application to a larger population or a different demographic. Not every study is generalizable, but generalizability is a hallmark of a strong and reliable methodology.

Chapter 66: Limitations

We all set out with the best of intentions and for whatever reason, we may fall short through no fault of our own. In Chapter One, you listed some limitations and delimitations you thought you might encounter. But in Chapter Five you will discuss those that you have encountered that were unexpected. Examples might include subjects dropping out (mortality), or a treatment that didn't go as planned, and may have been dropped. Conditions such as weather or other external factors that may have changed the methodology or the outcome would be other examples. Don't go back into Chapter One and add these occurrences as limitations, just mention them in Chapter Five and describe what went wrong and its effect on the study.

Chapter 67: Implications

You should summarize your study with your thoughts on what the research means to your field, the academic community, and the world at large. By stating this you are justifying your research as significant and worth the time and effort you put forth, not to mention the time of your committee and all who will read your research. It may also inform them that your research is a starting point that is worth using as a stepping stone for future efforts. For example, your study may open up a whole new line of research, a new way of doing the research (and possibly present opportunities for research funding).

Chapter 68: Suggestions for Future Research

Now that you have finished your current study, you now have an opportunity in this chapter to set up future research along this line. What did you find that was worth pursuing further? What answers yielded more questions? Better yet, what fertile ground have you cultivated that might provide funding for future research? Here is the place to make your case.

Chapter 69: Wrapping it Up

The closing section should remind the reader of what you have done ("Tell them what you told them"), and provide them with a "take away" message that will plant a memory of your research. You want this memory to stick firm enough so that when any topic related to yours comes up in daily conversation, those who have read your dissertation will remember your work and expertise, and perhaps will think of you as a "go to" person when they need to consult that expertise.

Chapter 70: References

The Reference section is probably one of the most time consuming details in the finalization of the dissertation. They don't have to be difficult, however. Keeping a running reference section as you write and cite, checking the APA (or style manual for your particular program) for each type of reference (book, journal, web, media, etc), and keeping things cross referenced as you write will help a lot. There are several software applications out there that claim to do the citing and proper reference formatting for you. Be careful. I have yet to find one without bugs. This includes the tool within MS Word and EndNote. Also, don't be lazy. Cite your sources fresh. Do not cut and paste from another paper. It could be wrong or not in accordance with the current version of your publishing guide (APA, MLA, etc), or the case of web references, they may move, be taken down or be given a new URL address. Do not rely on your committee to spot format errors. There is a possibility errors will be caught in the Form and Style review (More on form and style later), but I wouldn't count on it. Ultimately it is your paper. Get it right. Make it something to be proud of.

Chapter 71: Appendices

Supporting documentation for data contained within the paper can be inserted in the appendices.

Among the items found there might be:

Letters of Permission from the Research Sites

Informed Consent

IRB approval letter

other supporting documentation

Some people insert the raw surveys or other data sheets. This is not necessary unless your committee requires it. The trend now is to save trees by not including the raw data in the appendices. When in doubt, as always, consult your committee chair.

Chapter 72: Dedication and Acknowledgements

The one section where you have almost complete freedom are in the dedication and acknowledgement pages. The Dedication is usually a one or two liner on its own page. It can be to anybody you choose.

The Acknowledgements section is usually not more than two pages and you can use it to make statements, thank your committee, family, friends, lovers, anybody you want. I consider the one I wrote in my dissertation to be comedy gold. Look it up some time.

Chapter 73: Figures, Charts, and Tables

Figures are found within your paper, and can be any type of illustration that helps you clarify your statements. Charts are usually graphic depictions of data. You should keep in mind that charts and figures should not be in color unless your dissertation will be published electronically, or printed in color (this is not likely).

Finally, tables illustrate your data and are framed by textual descriptions. I have seen Results chapters built entirely with tables. Again only use tables that frame your results necessary to answer your Research Questions.

Chapter 74: The Table of Contents of the Dissertation

The Table of Contents is pretty much standardized. The format is strictly adhered to. There are tools within the popular word processing programs to insure proper formatting. The Table of Contents should be the last thing you construct in your dissertation. Major topic headings within the chapters should be all that appear in the Table of Contents. At the end should be References and Appendices. While the References will have a page number, Appendices will not (labeled as Appendix A, B, etc.) At the very bottom or on the next page you will list Tables, Figures, and Charts. Check your university dissertation manual, your writing center, and your committee to see if there are any local requirements that may differ from standard style manual.

Chapter 75: The Defense

You have already defended your proposal, so this meeting is not really unique, nor is it anything to worry about. If your committee has reviewed your dissertation and you revised accordingly, addressing all their concerns, then the meeting is pretty much an exercise. You will probably provide another presentation, similar to the one for your proposal, with the addition of the results and conclusions. Your committee may ask questions for clarification or just to keep you on your toes. Some schools have public defense meetings where the students and university community can attend. Some just have private meetings with the committee. Find out what your program does. Make sure the ground rules are known in advance. For example, is the audience allowed to ask questions in a public meeting? If you have a choice, avoid this as it leaves too many unknowns and unnecessarily prolongs the meeting. The questions often turn out to be the questioner showboating rather than posing a valid question. Remember, this is all about you. Don't let anybody hijack your day in the sun. When the committee has finished their questions, they will deliberate (ordinarily in private). They will vote to either approve outright, or with revision. Rarely, does disapproval take place at this point. Once you receive the verdict, you will receive further instructions from your chair as to what comes next and what forms are required, etc. Let me be the first to congratulate you. You are now officially a doctoral candidate, but remember, you are not yet a "Doctor" until the dissertation has gone through final university approval. Some universities don't allow candidates to use the letters after their name until the degree is confirmed. Check this out before you start handing out business cards with "Dr." in front of your name.

Chapter 76: Academic Review

The Academic Review, also called a Dean's Review or University Review, is a review by an appointed oversight person. This might be the Dean or Dean's representative, perhaps even a reviewer from outside your institution

It is not the nature of the review to contradict the committee, however, it does occur on occasion and when it does it often becomes a bone of contention in many programs. The review is intended to provide a "fresh set of eyes" in case something was missed or perhaps an error that had not been spotted previously. In many cases, a minor revision may be necessary, but upon the revision, the dissertation is usually signed and approved. It is best at this point to make the requested changes unless you have a solid rebuttal to the reviewer's comment. An argument will only delay approval unnecessarily. The reviewer is not there to play "gotcha", but to help you put out a solid product which reflects favorably upon you and the university. When the review is complete you are still not finished, however, there is one more step. That step is "Form and Style", which I will discuss in the next chapter.

Chapter 77: Form and Style

The Form and Style review is conducted usually by the writing center or a designated office within the university. It is intended to be final and format oriented. Here your columns, spacing, and punctuation will be reviewed. Some universities look at the style formatting (APA, MLA, etc), but this is usually complete by the time the dissertation reaches this point. Depending upon your university, you may have to complete recommended edits, or this may be done for you. Again, check your local dissertation manual, your chair, or graduate school office. This is the last step before publication. You are pretty much done. Again, congratulations!

Chapter 78: Copyright

Should you copyright your dissertation? If you plan on publishing any part of it in the future or claiming this as your intellectual property, then you should. There are certain forms of intellectual property protection. There is the copyright, which protects your work under the law and there is a relatively new protection called "Creative Commons". This protection is quite loose and provides open access to your work, as long as the person who uses it gives you credit (attribution). It is where much open source work is heading nowadays. Talk to your graduate school and chair as to what the norm is at your university, and what best works in your case.

Chapter 79: Publication

The old hard cover bound dissertation is becoming a thing of the past, although it is still the primary artifact used. Today you may see electronic dissertations, web based, and perhaps hyperlinked with audio and video files. Some may be a creative work ready for sale as a novel or non-fiction book. There are as many types of artifacts as there are types of dissertations and the options are growing every day as technology advances. Whatever format your work is published in, be proud of your work. You have produced a major scholarly effort that few people in the world have taken on, and much fewer have completed.

Chapter 80: Presenting your Work

So now that you have finished this opus, do you just throw it on a shelf to sit and collect dust? No, of course not. You want to show the world what you have accomplished. This is where you capsulize your study, prepare a summary in the form of slides, video, poster, or other media, and present it. You can present at conferences in person, virtually, or recorded for the web. These presentations can help you find a position, or provide lines on your vitae for promotion and tenure should you already be employed. There are ways you can take parts of your dissertation and present them separately, each one counting as a separate line on your vitae. Be creative. Talk to your committee. Ask them what they did with their dissertations. Go to conferences. Talk to presenters. If you have a fear of public speaking, consider a poster presentation or record a presentation for the web. Don't let fear stop you from reaping the fruits of your labor.

Chapter 81: Tailoring your dissertation into publishable articles.

In the previous chapter, I discussed taking parts of your dissertation and breaking it into separate presentations. This can also be done with journal articles. You can present the entire dissertation's results in a nutshell. You can write an article for each research question. You can write an article based on the literature review. You can even write an article discussing the answers you DIDN'T get!

Articles range from 3-20 pages, so you have plenty of opportunities to submit several articles. Talk with people in your field as to which articles should be submitted where and where you have the best chances to be published and where you might have the most impact. Look at the submission guidelines to the journals that you reviewed when you performed your review of the literature. The opportunities are almost endless.

Chapter 82: Publicity and Dissemination of your Research

Using the Public Relations office of your university or workplace is an excellent way of getting publicity for your work. Professional organizations, social networks, and getting on media expert lists are others. Here are some ways of publicizing your work:

-Write a blog

-A Facebook Page specifically for your work.

-A twitter account

-Getting in touch with radio stations (especially small public radio) to get on their experts list. They often call local people with expertise for interviews or to get a comment on particular stories.

-Free workshops- Conduct a few (emphasis on the word "few") workshops in your area of expertise. This can be done for a school district, for the community at the public library, or other setting.

There are many ways to get your work and your name out there. Keep your eyes open as to what your colleagues are doing. You never know where it may lead.

Chapter 83: Using your Dissertation to Drive your Career.

Hopefully, you have planned your dissertation in a manner that would pay dividends in your present job or pave the way for a future position. Having a published dissertation gives you a certain level of expertise in the niche that was your research area. You can use that expertise to obtain funding through grants, to build a reputation that may not only get you hired, but lead to employees actually looking to hire you away from your current employer. Finally, your dissertation, the presentations, and articles drawn from it, in addition to any follow-on research, will build your tenure and promotion file. You have laid the foundation. Now build on it.

Chapter 84: Closing comments

I would like to congratulate you for embarking on the research process, and thank you for reading this book. I will be producing videos and resources in the near future that I will be making available to all my readers. I am also available for consultation via email, Skype, or face to face. Finally, I hope to start conducting Smart Doctor workshops at several locations later in the year. Contact me at nolantextandvirtual@gmail.com with any questions and I will try to get back to you as soon as I can. I hope this book served you well in facilitating your dissertation completion or at least cleared up some confusion you may have had about the dissertation process. If you enjoyed the book, please leave feedback on the site where you purchased this book. Thanks again and good luck in your future pursuits.

Joseph E. Nolan, PhD

Appendix A: Research Plan Template

Introduction

Problem Statement

Purpose Statement

Nature of the Study

Research Questions

Hypotheses (or Objectives)

Variables (if applicable)

Population and sample

Appendix B: Dissertation Outline

The outline for the dissertation proposal and the dissertation are essentially identical for the first three chapters. This outline is based on the traditional five chapter study format. The following outline is provided as a sample that may be modified by the dissertation committee based upon demonstrated need of the scholarly project.

Abstract

Chapter 1: Introduction
Central theme/Background
Statement of the problem
Purpose of the study/project
Need for the study/project
Research questions
Hypothesis (Quantitative) or Objectives (Qualitative) of the project
Definition of terms

Chapter 2: Review of the Literature
Introduction
Theoretical Framework

Thorough review of relevant empirical studies and/or qualitative research

Summary

Chapter 3: Methodology (Quantitative or Qualitative)

Quantitative:

Research Design

Population and sample or participants

Instrumentation

Procedures

Data Analysis

Qualitative:

Research Design

Participants

Role of Researcher

Information Collection

Procedures

Information Analysis

Chapter 4: Data Analysis and Results

Data analysis and results, organized according to the research question(s)

Chapter 5: Conclusions

Findings or interpretation of results

Generalizations

Limitations

Implications

Suggestions for Future Research

Summary

References and Appendices

About the Author

Joseph E. Nolan has taught Research Methods for 18 years and supervised Doctoral students at 6 universities. He is often looked upon to consult when students are having problems finishing their dissertations. A first generation college graduate and non-traditional student himself, he knows about the obstacles that students face and how to overcome them.

When not teaching, he spends his time in Michigan, Texas, and Canada.

Made in the USA
Columbia, SC
05 February 2022